P9-ARL-974

Captions

Portrait of Emperor Qin Shi Huang   7

Foreword   8

The First Emperor of China   8

National Treasures See Daylight Again   11

The Unparalleled Grand Mausoleum   14

The Emperor's Chariot — State of the Art of Bronzeware   17

Three Armies Gather, Ready for War   19

A Great Book of Ancient Military Strategy   22

Realistic Sculpture   26

Emperor Qin Shi Huang's Mausoleum   28

Battle Formations of the Terracotta Army   30

Lifelike Statues   60

A Great Variety of Vivid Facial Expressions   86

Exquisite Craftsmanship with an Eye for Detail   103

Threatening, Sharp Weapons   108

Bronze Chariots and Horses of Superb Craftsmanship   112

Foreword

This is a myth left by history. When society has already entered the age of high-tech and computers, an army of powerful imperial soldiers clad in armor and wielding threatening sharp weapons suddenly looms out of the fog of time. As mysterious as extraterrestrial beings, the terracotta soldiers are at the same time so lifelike and real. They have come up again out of the earth, under which they had remained buried and unknown for more than 2,200 years. Was it because they could no longer bear the darkness and loneliness underground, or because they wanted to show people their ancient glory, long forgotten by time, or was it because Emperor Qin Shi Huang had, before his death, intended to demonstrate to later generations his absolute imperial power... For whatever reason, the re-appearance of his legions has given people the impression that the story of China is a book never to be fully read or understood. The many mysteries of the land of the Great Wall compel historians and archaeologists alike to search for explanations. The following is one of the most ancient, and yet true, stories.

1. The First Emperor of China

About 300 years after Sakyamuni, the founder of Buddhism, was born in what is now India, a baby boy was born in Handan, an ancient town in northern China. His first cry was no different from that of any other baby. Several decades later, however, he became a man to create new world and a person to be commemorated in history. The founder of the first unified empire in the history of China, as well as its first emperor, he was Emperor Qin Shi Huang. Two thousand years have since passed, but the name of Qin Shi Huang has been kept alive in the mind of all Chinese, just as the name of Napoleon rings out to the French and tales of the Pyramids still enchant modern Egyptians. Politicians have taken an interest in his political ambitions, gains and losses; ordinary people are more interested in his unusual life. His life and his political career are indeed still obscure.

The family name of Qin Shi Huang was Ying, and his given name was Zheng. He was born in 259 B.C. and died in 210 B.C. The early years of Ying Zheng's life were set against the last years of the Warring States Period, in which seven states, Qi, Chu, Yan, Han, Zhao, Wei and Qin, fought endlessly with each other in order to gain supreme authority. Ying Zheng's father, Zi Chu, was the grandson of King Zhao of the Qin Kingdom

and the son of King Anguo. At that time as a token of trust among states it was a common practice for kings in China to send one of their sons or grandsons to another kingdom as hostage. Among King Anguo's many offspring, Zi Chu was not the son of the Qin queen, nor was he the eldest son. Therefore he never enjoyed substantial prestige at the Qin court. When the relationship between Qin and Zhao deteriorated, Zi Chu was sent to Zhao as a hostage, where he led a hard and difficult life. Longing for home, each day seemed to him to last a year. Lü Buwei, a rich merchant in Handan, the capital of the Zhao Kingdom, was a man of political as well as practical foresight. Seeing the special background and circumstances of Zi Chu, Lü believed him a good investment and a hedge against future political upheavals. Therefore he spent a lot of money to pursuade local authorities to let Zi Chu go home. In addition, he gave Zhao Ji, one of his favorite concubines, to Zi Chu as his wife. Zhao Ji was a true beauty, good at the more refined arts of entertaining a husband. Not long afterward Zhao Ji gave birth to a son, who was given the name Ying Zheng. According to *Records of the Historian*, before Zhao Ji was married to Zi Chu, she was already pregnant by Lü Buwei. For this reason, who the biological father of Qin Shi Huang really was has remained an unsolved question. Some say he was indeed a natural son of Lü Buwei, and even say he should be called Lü Zheng. However, the circumstances of his birth did not, at any rate, affect his great contributions to history.

When Zi Chu returned to Qin to become king, he was enthroned as Zhuang Xiang and designated Ying Zheng as his heir. When King Zhuang Xiang died after a long illness in 246 B.C., Ying Zheng became the Qin king. He was only 13, too young to administrate state affairs or to comprehend the complicated political and military problems of the time. The power of Qin actually lay in the hands of Lao Ai, his mother's favorite courtier, and the prime minister Lü Buwei. When Ying Zheng turned 22

years old in 238 B.C., he was formally crowned at Qinian Palace and thereupon bagan to handle state affairs himself. The young and ambitious Ying Zheng had long been dissatisfied with the regency of Prime Minister Lü and Lao Ai. Now that he had real power, he had Lao Ai murdered, his mother put under house arrest and Lü Buwei dismissed from his post. He solicited outside advice and promoted a new elite of both civil and military officials, including the mandarins Li Si and Wang Wan, and the generals Wang Jian, Wei Liao and Meng Tian. Ying then carried out the reforms advocated by his father, developing agriculture and the military. Soon Qin became the strongest of the seven warring states, defeating on the battlefield and through Machiavellian diplomacy the other six states from 230 to 221 B.C. Han, Zhao, Yan, Wei, Chu and Qi all fell, one by one, victims of Qin's alliances and orchestration of diplomatic intrigue and isolation. China's division of more than several hundred years, lasting since the Spring and Autumn Period, came to an end and, for the first time in history, China became a unified, multi-nationality empire under a central government. After unification, Ying Zheng ordered his ministers to discuss possible titles for a supreme ruler of the country and a suitable name for the empire. Although the ministers suggested many titles and names, Ying Zheng decided his virtue and contribution to the country were greater than all previous kings and chieftains. Therefore the supreme ruler of the country should be called the emperor, with he himself naturally being the first emperor - Shi Huang. Thereafter for 2,000 years, "emperor" remained the official title for the supreme political authority in China. To consolidate his power, Qin Shi Huang abolished the fiefdoms of the Shang and Zhou dynasties, and divided the country into 36 prefectures, broken down further into counties, townships, *ting*s and *li*s. The central government had 12 ministers directly responsible to the emperor and the majority of military and administrative officials were all directly appointed or removed by the

emperor himself. Thus Emperor Qin Shi Huang had both the military and administrative powers of China concentrated in his hands. He ordered the establishment of new laws, by which "everything was to be dictated." Law became an important institution in China by which the emperor asserted his authority. Qin Shi Huang was also responsible for the "three unifications:" 1. Unification of weights and measures. 2. Unification of the Chinese written language, through the use of the official script of the Qin State across the country, under the auspices of Prime Minister Li Si and the mandarin Zhao Gao. 3. Unification of currency, involving abolition of the currencies of the former six kingdoms in exchange for Qin coins.

These measures were significant for the economic and cultural development of China, setting the stage for one of the world's great civilizations. Other projects completed under Qin Shi Huang included a network of roads and the linking up of the defensive walls and fortifications previously built by the seven old warring states. Thus came into being the 10,000-*li* Great Wall of China, starting from Lintao in the west and ending at Shanhaiguan Pass in the east. Many still praise Qing Shi Huang as "the most outstanding emperor for a thousand years." All his life, indeed, he was busy creating wonders.

In 210 B.C. Qin Shi Huang died of illness at the age of 50 at Pingtai, in Shaqiu (the present-day Guangzong County of Hebei Province) while on an inspection tour of his empire. After Qin Shi Huang's death, his younger son Hu Hai usurped the throne by changing the imperial verdict and murdering his elder brother Fu Su. Hu Hai crowned himself as Qin Er Shi, or the Second Emperor of Qin. The Qin Empire, however, had already enjoyed its heyday. Not long afterward a peasant uprising led by Chen Sheng and Wu Guang destroyed the Qin Dynasty, which had been in power only 15 years. Thus the earliest dynasty of China was also one of its most brief. What accounted for its quick fall? First, the Qin

rulers had merciless laws and punishments for offenders. There were, for instance, several dozen different death penalities and corporal punishments, many of them indescribably ruthless. The network of laws was pervasive and unforgiving. From high officials and aristocrats to the ordinary people, everybody was subject to some sort of accusation if they did not act cautiously. Lu Jia of the Han Dynasty criticized Qin rule as "applying too many and too cruel a set of penalties." Second, corvée labor and taxes were very predominant under the Qin Dynasty. According to estimates based on historic records, in the first 10 years of China's unification, 500,000 soldiers were sent to guard the mountains in southern China, 500,000 laborers were recruited to build the Great Wall, 300,000 troops were stationed in the north against the Xiongnu tribes, 700,000 men were engaged in the construction of the E'fang Palace and the mausoleum for Emperor Qin Shi Huang. These and other projects, all using corvée labor, involved a total of more than 2 million people, 10 percent of China's population at the time. Since most of the laborers were young males, the productive forces of Chinese society suffered considerably, not to mention those families liable for forced labor or heavy taxes. Third, the sheer incompetence of Qin Er Shi was also a large factor in the fall of the dynasty. In fact, he was so stupid as to trust treacherous courtiers, and reputedly paid no mind to the words of honest officials.

The rise and decline of the Qin Dynasty has always been a popular subject of research for Chinese politicians and historians. The fifty years that Emperor Qin Shi Huang walked on the earth has also remained a subject of controversy for later generations. There is praise as well as criticism, and this discussion is very likely to continue. The fact that Emperor Qin Shi Huang's merits and failings have aroused so much debate in the past 2,000 years shows he occupied an especially important place in Chinese history, and was, for better or for worse, one of China's great men.

The landscape of Pit No. 2 before excavation.

The landscape of Pit No. 3 before excavation.

2. National Treasures See Daylight Again

Many important and wonderful pages in the lore of archaeology were written quite by accident with the discovery of the terracotta warriors and horses of the Qin Dynasty as a typical example. The people to make this discovery were several ordinary Chinese farmers.

It started out like any other day in early spring 1974, when Yang Peiyan, Yang Zhifa and Yang Wenxue from the village of Xiyang, in Lintong County in Shaanxi, began to dig a well in the persimmon grove to the south of the village. The well would hopefully provide water during the coming spring drought. On the fifth day, their shovels struck a layer of extremely hard earth, which was red and seemed to have been baked or fired. None of the farmers knew what to do next, and their arms and hands were already quite sore from the resilient force of this strange and stubborn wall transmitted through the picks. After digging another three to four meters down, they noticed some peculiar pottery fragments and a jar-like container. The farmers became very careful, for if the jar turned out to be intact they could have then recycled it and used it to store eggs. The more they dug, the more their find appeared to be the thoracic cavity of what the locals called a "pottery man." The head, arms and legs of the "pottery man" soon became visible, and with it some rusted bronze triggers of crossbows, arrowheads and floor tiles.

The three men still had no idea what they were digging up. The most logical conclusion was that it was an old kiln for bricks and tiles of some sort, while other more superstitious types figured it could be a temple to the God of Earth. Others suggested that the "pottery man" was an underground arhat. But would it bring good or bad luck to the village? Nobody could tell for sure. Some of the more elderly locals, fearful that they had accidentally

Terracotta warriors and horses.

unearthed the statue of a god, secretly burned incense and kowtowed to the heavens to pray for forgiveness. The small village, usually quiet, became restless. It so happened that Lao Fang, a cadre in charge of water resources, came to the village on the day of the discovery to inspect progress on the new well. He took a good look at the digging site. The floor tiles reminded him of an old tomb site several kilometers away. "Look," he said, turning to the villagers, "don't these tiles look like the ones unearthed near the Qin Shi Huang Mau-

soleum?" It dawned then and there on everybody that they had discovered some sort of ancient burial site. They immediately stopped digging and reported the news to the county government.

From Lintong County, the news went to Xi'an and then to Beijing. With government approval, an archaeological team from Shaanxi Province arrived in July 1974, and the most momentous archaeological excavations of the 20th century were soon under way.

In 1976, after two years of initial explorations, the team reached the conclusion that the site could only be terracotta warriors and horses buried with Qin Shi Huang, the first emperor of China. Three pits were discovered, with a total area of more than 20,000 square meters. Unearthed were nearly 8,000 terracotta warriors and horses and more than 100 wooden war chariots.

Thus an archaeological wonder was brought to light, and an imperial army came back to life.

Many years after the discovery, journalists who went to interview the local villagers came across some interesting stories. When the farmers brought the broken pottery warrior they had dug up at the well site on a cart to the county cultural relics administrative department, they were given 30 yuan as compensation for their delayed work as well as a small reward. The farmers were very pleased, and although it was a fairly small sum it did not cross their minds to demand more money. They were content enough with the fame their discovery had brought to Xiyang. Some older folk related even earlier discoveries in their childhood. Whenever their fathers or uncles unearthed a pottery warrior while digging a well or grave, it was regarded as an ominous sign. They would, to assuage their fears and superstitions, either hang the clay warrior up to be whipped, leave it out to disintegrate in the sun, or break it into pieces and rebury the fragments deep in the earth. Nobody had ever imagined the clay figures were historical relics, let alone try to figure out their worth to China and to historians worldwide.

Discovery of the three pits came as a shock to the country as well as to the whole world. From 1974 to date, tens of millions of visitors from China and abroad have visited the terracotta legions of Emperor Qin Shi Huang. Lee Kuan Yew, the former prime minister of Singapore, praised them as a "wonder of the world and (a source of) pride for the nation." Dr. Henry Kissinger, the former U.S. Secretary of State, visited the site three times, saying that he was "deeply impressed by the terracotta warriors and horses of the Qin Dynasty, unique and unparalleled in the world." He noted that "a nation that could create such a great history and culture will certainly create a brighter future." When the former French premier Jacques Chirac visited the terracotta pits in 1978, he wrote that "there are already seven wonders in the world. The terracotta pits can be regarded as the eighth. You can't come to China without seeing the terracotta warriors and horses, just as you can't go to Egypt without visiting the pyramids." His comments and the observation of other visitors soon spread far and wide. Today "the eighth wonder of the world" has almost become synonymous with the terracotta soldiers of the Qin Dynasty.

While marveling at the legions and chariots, visitors often raise many questions. Who built these pits? When were they built? What did they symbolize? What was the relationship between the pits and Emperor Qin Shi Huang's mausoleum? Who later set fire to the pits? To answer any of these questions, we must go backways, more than 2,000 years ago.

Let us start from Emperor Qin Shi Huang's mausoleum.

3. The Unparalleled Grand Mausoleum

Emperor Qin Shi Huang's mausoleum is located about 7.5 kilometers east of Lintong County in Shaanxi Province. It is faced by Mount Li to the south and bordered by the Wei River to the north. It is believed that Emperor Qin Shi Huang selected this site for his mausoleum because of the scenery. In addition, Mount Li was very rich in gold and jade deposits. According to legend, "the southern side (of Mount Li) produces gold while the northern side produces jade. Emperor Qin Shi Huang loved this beautiful place and so decided to be buried here." Today the mausoleum is not only under key state protection, but has become the only imperial mausoleum in China to receive UNESCO recognition as part of its world cultural heritage program.

In Chinese history, almost all emperors paid special attention to two things. One was to try all means of gaining immortality, and, failing this, to at least build a grand mausoleum. Immortality was, of course, difficult in the best of times. Therefore an opulent mausoleum became the preoccupation of many who sat on the Dragon Throne. According to historical records, Emperor Qin Shi Huang sent thousands of virgin boys and girls, led by the legendary Xu Fu, out to sea looking for the divine islands of Penglai, Fangzhang and Yingzhou, said to hold the elixirs of immortality. He organized several such expeditions, all the while knowing that man was mortal anyway. He began his mausoleum project at Mount Li as soon as he ascended to the Qin throne.

Many historical documents still exist to tell us about the construction of Emperor Qin Shi Huang's mausoleum, how long it took and how it originally appeared on the inside. Starting with the description of Sima Qian (about 145 or 135 B.C.-?), the great Han Dynasty historian known for his realistic records of historical events, "Shi Huang began building his mausoleum soon after he became king of Qin. After the unification of the whole country, more than 700,000 slaves were sent to work on the mausoleum. The burial chamber was deep underground, and the catafalque for the coffin was cast of copper. Palaces were built in the burial chamber, home to countless rare treasures. Artisans were instructed to build hidden crossbows, which would automatically shoot arrows if thieves approached the tomb. Mercury was mechanically poured into the tomb to form rivers and seas of poison. The ceiling was adorned with the sun, the moon and stars, and laid out on the earth were landscapes of places from across the country. Candles made from the fat of mermaids were lighted to burn forever. At the order of Emperor Qin Er Shi, those concubines of the former Emperor who did not bear any children, and who were not suitable to leave the royal palace, were buried alive with the Emperor. Thus many died as human burial objects. Some say that since the artisans and architects knew the passageways and treasures of the tomb too well themselves, they would tell others the secret of the mausoleum if they were so allowed... To avoid this, channels and walkways inside the tomb were quickly sealed after the ceremony, and pathways leading to the outside were also closed up. Not a single man was let out. Afterward grass and trees were planted on the surface of the tomb, disguising it as a mound..." According to this passage, from Sima's biography of "Emperor Qin Shi Huang" in the *Records of the Historian*, construction of the mausoleum began in 246 B.C., and the whole project was completed only after his death, indicating a time span of approximately 38 years. The number of corvée laborers mobilized was more than 700,000, an astounding figure for the time. The scale and cost of Emperor Qin Shi Huang's mausoleum were probably larger than that of the pyramid of the Egyptian Pharoah Hufu, and stands as proof of Emperor Qin Shi Huang's extreme extravagance.

But then, to what extent can we believe the

An excavation site.

records of Sima Qian? In order to find the answer to the secret of Emperor Qin Shi Huang's final resting place, archaeologists began to study the mausoleum through explorative digs in the early 1960s. New revelations show that the original mausoleum mound was about 115 meters high, in a shape closely resembling a square, or an upside-down square cap. More than 2,000 years of erosion by wind and rain and additional damage caused by the carelessness of man have reduced the mound today to a height of 76 meters. The base of the mausoleum is 345 meters from east to west and 350 meters from north to south, rather like a pyramid. Originally two rectagular walls surrounded the tomb mound. The inner wall was 1,355 meters from north to south and 580 meters from east to west, with a perimeter of 3,870 meters, while the outer wall was 2,165 meters from north to south and 940 meters from east to west, with a perimeter of 6,210 meters. Most of the walls have long since col-

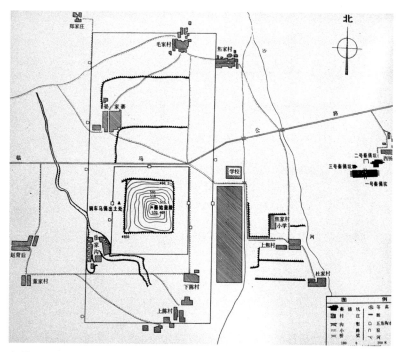

A diagram of Emperor Qin Shi Huang's mausoleum and the pits of terracotta warriors and horses.

the design and overall layout of the mausoleum of Emperor Qin Shi Huang. Archaeological digs have unearthed a large number of attendant burial pits and tombs around the mausoleum. So far more than 400 such pits and tombs, covering an area of 56.25 square kilometers, have been discovered, yielding some 50,000 invaluable cultural artifacts over the years. Some tombs contained bronze horse-drawn chariots, built in imitation of the Emperor's chariots; in other pits there have been found terracotta birds and animals, symbolizing the Emperor's love for hunting; some other pits housed replicas of the imperial stable. Everthing known to the emperor was buried with him after his death. These finds, combined with historical records, indicate Emperor Qin Shi Huang's mausoleum was actually a miniature replica of the Qin Empire. The terracotta warriors and horses, an important part of the mausoleum, were to guard the Qin Empire after Qin Shi Huang's passing, with the emperor enjoying status, even in death, as supreme ruler of the realm. Mortality was not to stop him from enjoying an extravagant life and command of the mightiest army known to the world at that time.

Archaeological studies have proved that the pits containing the terracotta warriors and horses were built during the same period as the mausoleum. To be more precise, they were built from 221 to 210 B.C., from the unification of China up to the death of the Emperor. But experts have different ideas as to the cause for and time of the fire that swept through the pits. Some say the fire was caused by the ignition of methane deposits underground. Some believe the pits were burned as part of the burial ceremony. But most archaeologists who have participated in the excavation believe the pits were burned in 206 B.C. by the rebellious troops of Xiang Yu, a conclusion supported by some of the writings of Sima Qian. A few of the unearthed warriors also show that this may have been likely, and this particular hypothesis has therefore been accepted by many.

lapsed, leaving behind the remains of an 8-meter-wide base. The outer wall had gates leading out in all four directions, and the inner wall had two gates on the northern side and one gate on each remaining side, with a guard tower at every corner. Three sets of ruins, presumably small palaces of some sort, have been discovered within the confines of the walls. They were most likely ceremonial sites and living quarters for the tomb guards. Modern testing has confirmed that the central part of the mausoleum still contains miniscule traces of mercury over an estimated area of 12,000 square meters, proving Sima Qian's record of "mercury forming rivers and seas."

So many buildings that were above ground have been reduced to ruins or have simply vanished without a trace that it is difficult to determine what the original mausoleum might have looked like. But the number of unusually well-preserved relics beneath the ground have provided archaeologists with a good idea as to

4. The Emperor's Chariot — State of the Art of Bronzeware

After the discovery of the terracotta legions, another significant excavation unearthed two painted bronze chariots, remarkably realistic in structure and detail, of the imperial court. They were originally buried 20 meters west of the Emperor's mausoleum, placed one after the other facing west in a large wooden coffin about 7 meters long and 2.3 meters wide. Both chariots and the horses drawing them were half scale, presumably for the use of the dead Emperor on an outing in the afterlife. The two chariots are now on display in a special hall at the Emperor Qin Shi Huang's Terracotta Museum, numbered 1 and 2 according the order in which they were discovered. Each chariot has two wheels, and a single shaft attached to four bronze horses. But they also differ in some respects. According to the Han Dynasty historian Cai Yong, they were both service vehicles for the Emperor's chariots. No. 1 chariot was responsible for clearing the road for the Emperor's entourage. The oblong coach box is 126 centimeters from side to side and 70 centimeters from back to front, with a bronze umbrella, 122 centimeters in diameter, under which stands a bronze imperial guard, a long and threatening sword at his side. Other details to the chariots include a pair of bronze shields, a crossbow and arrow, and a box containing 66 bronze arrowheads. The horses, each about 90 centimeters tall and 110 centimeters long, are painted white. There are gold and silver halters on the heads of all the horses, with tassels hanging down the necks. The horses have on both sides gold and silver reins, and on the forehead of the right one there is an army banner, showing that the horses belong to the imperial court. All four have cut mane and plaited tails, with their heads positioned high and looking forward, and the legs poised to gallop, creating an air of might and vigilance. The second chariot is a sleeping chariot. The horses and chariot all together are 3.17 meters long, 1.06 meters tall and weigh 1,241 kilograms. The coach box is composed of two parts. Looking at it from above, it is in the shape of a " 凸 ." In front is the charioteer's position with a special enclosure in back, complete with a door and three windows, for the rider. The windows, made of wood, have small holes in them to screen the rider from sun, wind, sand and dust, while allowing him to to see the landscape outside. The sliding windows can be opened and closed easily. The square chariot is covered by an oval arched roof, symbolizing the round sky and the square earth in line with the ancient Chinese belief about the shape of the universe. The bronze charioteer in front of the carriage, in a sitting position, is 51 centimeters tall, clothed in a long garment and a cap decorated with feathers. He is represented as concentrating on his driving, with a smile almost as an afterthought, perhaps to represent pride in his high position. But his expression shows that he is also nervous, as one must always be in the presence of the emperor.

The Shang Dynasty was the golden age of bronze in China. People believed that as iron came more and more into use, the bronze culture declined, to disappear almost entirely by the Qin and Han dynasties. The Qin Dynasty bronze horses and chariots, when first discovered, forced some reconsideration of this opinion. The works show an incredible level of artistic achievement at the end of China's bronze age. Another revelation of the Qin Dynasty horses and chariots was the use of color so early in the history of Chinese art. On the roof and body of the two chariots are designs of clouds, dragons and phoenixes, all portrayed in bright colors. Elsewhere there are gold and silver squares, rhombuses and triangles, finely drawn. The majority of these motifs are splendidly done, sedate and graceful while showing a high level of bronze craftsmanship. The first chariot is composed of 3,064 spare parts, the second of 3,462. Each includes more than 1,000 pieces of gold and silver, assembled through the various casting,

welding, chiseling, polishing and inlaying techniques invented by Qin Dynasty craftsmen. Many parts of the chariots are overlaid with chains fashioned from extremely fine copper wire, some strands only 0.05 centimeters in diameter. Viewed under a microscope the wires show no sign of having been forged, meaning that they could have only been stretched and drawn out to the desired attenuation before welded into rings and chains. There are other practical and technically impressive touches on the chariots as well. On No. 1 chariot there is a spare part for fixing the umbrella. By slightly moving a key, the lock to the umbrella opens, and when locked, the umbrella is firmly planted in a hole of the lock. This device shows us the skill and ingenuity of the ancient craftsmen.

The bronze horses and chariots unearthed in Qin Shi Huang's burial chamber are the largest of all the Qin figures discovered so far as well as the most splendidly decorated, most lifelike and best preserved relics of their kind ever found in China. No other ancient bronzes can compare for intricacy and superb workmanship, and they stand as the best in the long tradition of Chinese bronzeware. They are also invaluable archaeological and historical pieces as examples of ancient chariots from early Chinese history, enabling us to imagine how impeccable the real horses and chariots of Emperor Qin Shi Huang must have been. It is not surprising that Liu Bang, before he became emperor, said with admiration upon seeing Emperor Qin Shi Huang's chariot procession, "This is the life a man should lead."

5. Three Armies Gather, Ready for War

The pits containing the terracotta pieces are about 1.5 kilometers east of Emperor Qin Shi Huang's mausoleum. The three pits are arranged in the shape of "品." They are called No. 1, No. 2 and No. 3, according to the order of discovery, and they are all underground wood-and-earth structures. A series of 5-meter-deep pits were first prepared, then foundations of rammed earth were laid down and separated by 3-meter-high walls. The ground then was laid over with black bricks, and the terracotta soldiers, horses and chariots were placed between the walls. On all sides of the pit and each side of the walls pillars were set up equidistant from one another, and then laid over with beams to support a roof of thick wooden planks. The planks were covered with mats, reddish clay and loess, and openings were made in the walls for each pit. Once the terracotta pieces were all in position, the openings were sealed, forming a sealed palace of sorts underground. The three pits are independent of each other, not connected by any passage. Yet in terms of Qin military strategy, the legions are meant to form a united army to guard the Emperor in the afterlife.

Pit No.1, the largest of the three, is 230 meters from east to west and 62 meters from north to south, occupying an area of 14,260 square meters. It has more than 6,000 terracotta soldiers and horses and some 40 wooden chariots. The legions are arranged in four groups: a vanguard, the main body, the flank and the rearguard. In front there are three rows of 204 infantrymen with no armor. Each row includes 68 figures precisely, each soldier having tied hair and bows and arrows ready in their hands. As they are supposed to be skilled bowmen, they are the Qin vanguard, serving in Qin strategy as the tip of the sword, sharp and cutting. Behind the vanguard, the pit is divided by walls into 11 sections with 38 columns of chariots and infantrymen. These soldiers

are wearing armor protection, with additional shields on the knees and for the neck. They wield spears and daggers, and a select few are using bows and arrows. The soldiers are accompanied by chariots to form a powerful main body. On the northern and southern sides of the pit, there are rows of warriors facing both directions, forming a flank to prevent enemy forces from attacking on both sides. In the rear there is a row of soldiers facing west, with their back to the main body. This is the rearguard, whose task is to prevent the enemy from sneaking up from behind. According to ancient military strategists the rearguard was like the handle of a sword, a very important role on the battlefield.

Pit No. 2, an L-shaped area, is 20 meters northeast of Pit No. 1. It is 124 meters from east to west and 98 meters from north to south, covering an area of about 6,000 square meters. Judging from the amount of exploratory digging and excavating that has already taken place, there are around 350 terracotta chariot horses, 116 cavalry horses and 900 soldiers of different kinds, for a total of 1,400 terracotta pieces and 89 wooden chariots, all in a military formation of four echelons. The first wave is composed of 230 or so archers in front of the main formation, 160 of whom are clad in armor and kneeling in 8 columns in the center; around them are 170 archers standing without armor protection, but clad in battle robes. Thus, when engaged in a battle, the two groups, one kneeling and the other standing, would deliver alternate volleys of arrows into enemy ranks. The second echelon, 64 chariots, is to the right of the bowmen. Each chariot carries a charioteer and two armored warriors, without infantry support. The third echelon, a mixture of 19 chariots, 8 cavalry members and 260 infantry, is in the middle of the formation. The final wave is to the left of the main formation and is composed of 108 cavalrymen and 6 chariots. The cavalrymen here are tall and stout, wearing leather hats and boots and armored suits, with a bow in one hand and reins in the other to give an appearance of agility and skill. The horses are well fed and

Outside view of the exhibition hall for Pit No. 3.

smartly equipped. The overall appearance is truly warlike, and is meant to portray the armies of Qin Shi Huang as a fearsome, courageous and swift opponent on the battlefield.

Pit No. 3, a " 凹 "-shaped area, is 25 meters to the northwest of Pit No. 1 and 120 meters to the east of Pit No. 2. Its total area is less than 500 square meters, the smallest of the three. Fewer pieces have been unearthed here, only 66 warriors, four horses and a sole wooden chariot. Despite its size, No. 3 is a more significant discovery than the other two pits. The soldiers have not been arranged in any military formation, but were simply left in two chambers facing north and south. The two rows are facing each other, weapons in hands.

Obviously they are the guards for battlefield headquarters. The pit also contains deer horns and animal bones used in sacrificial rites.

Even in the earliest days of Chinese civilization, armies were divided into the left, middle and right or upper, middle and lower echelons. So it was during the Qin Dynasty. Pit No. 1 consists of the right wing, No. 2 the left and No. 3 the headquarters. There is no middle echelon, however. Recent digs have uncovered another pit to the north of Pit No. 1 and west of Pit No. 2, with nearly the same shape and same depth as the other three. There are no clay soldiers or horses inside, however, just mud and sand accumulated through the ages. Hence this "phantom pit" is rarely mentioned,

Outside view of the exhibition hall for Pit No. 1.

but it is still possible, or so specialists think, that it was intended for the main echelon. Peasant uprisings and unrest towards the end of the Qin Dynasty meant that this pit could not be completed.

The pits, for all their size and impressiveness, are still just a miniature composite of a genuine Qin Dynasty army. One can still visit the site and feel the grandeur and power of the army of an ancient empire that existed over 2,000 years ago. The soldiers are all the more lifelike wielding their bronze weapons. Though only parts of the legions have been unearthed, more than 10 types of weapons, including swords, spears, daggers, axes, and arrows, totalling more than 30,000 examples of

nearly every Qin weapon known to historians, have been catalogued. The weapons show exquisite workmanship, with even shapes and sharp points and edges. The metallic alloy of each weapon is in the right proportion. After being buried for more than 2,000 years, they have lost none of their shine or sharpness. Examinations by electronic probe and laser microspectral tests show a layer of an oxidized chromium compound, an agent against rust and corrosion, on the surface of the weapons. This technique has been known to Western manufacturers in modern times, but apparently it was already in use in China 2,000 years ago, a true landmark in the history of metallurgy.

6. A Great Book of Ancient Military Strategy

The pits speak volumes about Qin military power. They provide an incredible amount of information of the distribution and formation of ranks on the field, the use of weapons, and overall tactics in ancient Chinese warfare.

During the Spring and Autumn Period and again in the Warring States Period, China was torn apart by rival kingdoms and states. Civilization was in a constant state of flux and warfare was the predominant way of life. It was a time for the emergence of advanced military science and in-depth study of the "art of war," producing in turn some of the first major treatises on warfare. *Master Sun's Art of War*, *Master Wu's Art of War* and *Sun Bin's Art of War*, practically bibles of the battlefield even to this day despite their sometimes obscure language and plethora of nuances and subtleties, all appeared at this time. Discovery of Qin Shi Huang's terracotta legions helped to resolve some passages in these texts which had been hitherto unclear.

Military formations are formed according to certain military principles and strategies. Whether a war is lost or won often depends on whether military formations are reasonable or not. Military formations can also reflect an army's power, and ancient military scientists stressed the importance of military formation. They advocated an agile vanguard leading a powerful main body into battle, with formation to be maintained throughout the engagement. A courageous warrior would never proceed alone, nor would a timid one retreat alone; in short, no one would break rank so long as order was maintained. This was a tenet brought up all throughout *Master Sun's Art of War*, and it was an ideal reflected in the layout of Qin Shi Huang's terracotta soldiers and chariots. There is a smart and nimble vanguard preceding an imposing main echelon, forming a mighty army which is invincible because it is so well ordered. Different troops and weapons have advantages and disadvantages in different scenarios, making it necessary to organize them in such a way as to bring their strengths into full play while avoiding their weak points. This is a simple yet vital principle again reflected among the terracotta legions. Pit No. 2 includes chariots, infantrymen, cavalrymen and archers. Among the infantrymen there are those with armor and those without armor. Chariots are included for the commander, as well as a chariot for his aide, chariots for three soldiers and chariots for four soldiers, each with a different purpose. It is mentioned in *Master Sun's Art of War* that when the battle is going to be an easy one more chariots should be used; when there are to be difficulties more horses will be needed, and when the danger is at its greatest archers should be employed *en masse*. A military formation composed of various kinds of soldiers can handle any situation that arises in battle to gain the upper hand. During the Battle of Changping between the Qin and Zhao states in 260 B.C., the Qin army used military formations of every kind of soldier and weapon available, and thereby slaughtered 400,000 Zhao soldiers and defeated the less innovative Zhao commanders. The huge number of cavalrymen and chariots unearthed show that Qin cavalry functioned as an independent force in battle, with chariots playing a vital strategic role. Previous opinions that use of chariots in battle had ceased with the end of the Warring States Period and the establishment of unified rule over China turned out to be wrong.

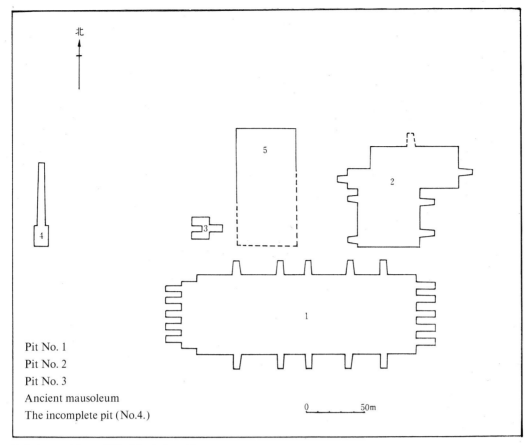

Pit No. 1
Pit No. 2
Pit No. 3
Ancient mausoleum
The incomplete pit (No.4.)

Relative positions of Pits No. 1, 2 and 3.

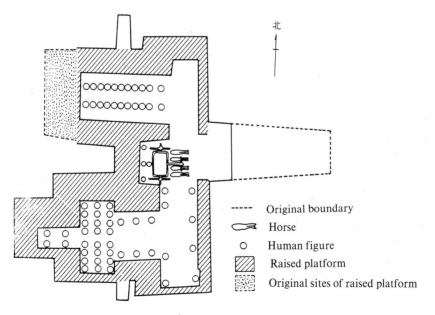

- - - - Original boundary

🐎 Horse

○ Human figure

▨ Raised platform

▦ Original sites of raised platform

Plan of the battle formation in Pit No. 3.

Plan of the battle formation in Pit No. 1.

Legend:

- ⊥ Chariot
- ♉ Horse
- ○ Robed warrior
- ◎ Armored soldier with round bun
- ⊕ Armored soldier with headdress
- ⊖ Armored soldier with flat bun
- ⊘ Officer
- ⊜ Charioteer
- ⊖ A serviceman
- ⊗ Soldiers with unknown hair-style

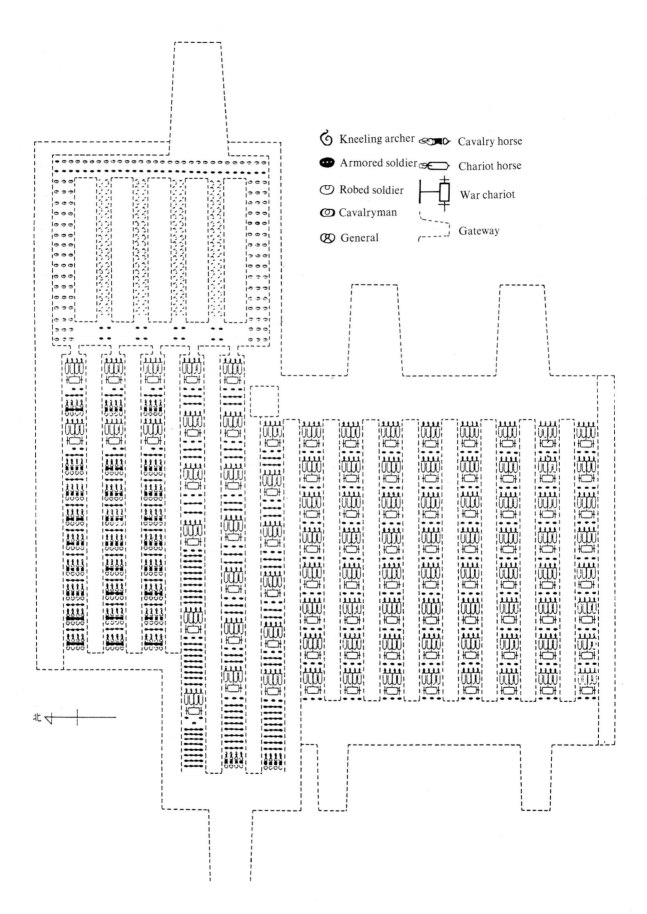

Kneeling archer   Cavalry horse

Armored soldier   Chariot horse

Robed soldier   War chariot

Cavalryman

General   Gateway

北

Plan of the battle formation in Pit No. 2.

7. Realistic Sculpture

The pits containing the terracotta pieces are more than a treasure trove for military historians, however. The legions of Qin Shi Huang are known in art museums and to connoisseurs the world over.

The terracotta soldiers, horses and chariots are on a scale so grand and immense that they remained unmatched to this day by other relics from the same period in history. The three pits include nearly 8,000 pottery soldiers and horses, still waiting for the command to attack. The soldiers are all around 1.8 meters tall, the tallest being 2 meters, and are all stoutly built. The horses are usually 2 meters long and 1.7 meters tall, the same dimensions as the real animal. The legions remain the only discovery of so great a number of life-sized horses in the history of Chinese archaeology.

The horses and soldiers are all true to life. The human figures are true to form and of the correct proportions, while the horses are muscular, have big, bright eyes, large noses and mouths, healthy, stout legs and plump waists and hips, ready to gallop. The terracotta human figures include generals, officers and soldiers, each with different dress and ornaments commensurate with rank and in different life-like gestures and poses. The generals, graceful and the picture of refinement and nobility, are tall, covered in gowns and colorful fish-scale armor accentuated by long caps and shoes with turned-up points and square openings. The officers wear gowns and armors, and are posed in various heroic and masculine countenances. Soldiers include infantrymen, cavalrymen, standing archers and kneeling archers. The kneeling archers have their left legs slightly bent, right legs on the ground, and are holding bows with both hands. The standing archers have their left legs stepped forward, slightly bent and the right legs straight, the two feet forming a "T." The left arms are streched forward and right arms held in front of the chests, in the typical shooting gesture. Each terracotta piece is an individual work of art, however, because, each human face is different and every warrior has a different expression. Some look very lively and entertained, some are serious and reserved, some look quite indignant and others are lost in thought. Some men are smiling, showing off their delicate features, while others have big eyes, sharp noses, and strong masculine features. It is even possible with some of the warriors to guess from their features and expressions their native place, age and personality. Some people have recognized among the soldiers peasants from the central Shaanxi plain, young men

from Sichuan and shepherds from the plains of northern China. They are all very lifelike.

Bright colors and pigments were applied to the terracotta pieces when first completed, but due to the fire that later swept through the pits and exposure to moisture, the colors have now faded. One can still see various shades of red, green, blue and brown, with touches of bright yellow, white and black coloring, all made from ground minerals. One can imagine that when the pits were completed, the warriors must have created a startling impression. Assuming that each of the 8,000 terracotta figures had 2 square meters of painted area, the whole painting project would have been equal to a huge painting of 15 kilometers long and 1 meter wide, quite a remarkable achievement.

The figures also show an exquisite technique and advanced craftsmanship in pottery. The pits contain a huge number of terracotta pieces, each one fairly large. It is a hard process from first fashioning the clay body to the final firing in the kiln. After careful examination it was discovered that sculpting, with some molding as needed, was used. There was a whole set of traditional techniques used, including hand-shaping, carving and painting. The rough body of legs and feet were hand shaped, then sculpted. The torso was also hand-shaped, then gowns and armor were sculpted and detailed. Making the heads was a very complicated process, requiring first a rough form of the head cast in a mold. The plaited hair and buns were then fashioned from extra clay spread on the cast, followed by the ears and the neck, which were first made separately, then luted on. The eyes, nose, mouth and hair strands were brought out by careful carving and incising. The horses were made in more or less the same fashion. First the different parts of the body were created, then sealed together to form a rough outline. More clay was applied to the surface and the fine details carved. The combination of different techniques was not only efficient but also allowed for a variety of human figures. Tests and analysis show that the pieces were fired at a temperature between 950 to 1050°C. Most of them emerged pure in color, extremely hard and quite durable. All signs indicate that they were fired with a degree of skill which experimental firings even today have not been able to replicate.

Simply for their superb artistry and vigorous style, if not more, the terracotta figures of Qin Shi Huang are of everlasting artistic value.

Emperor Qin Shi Huang's

Mausoleum

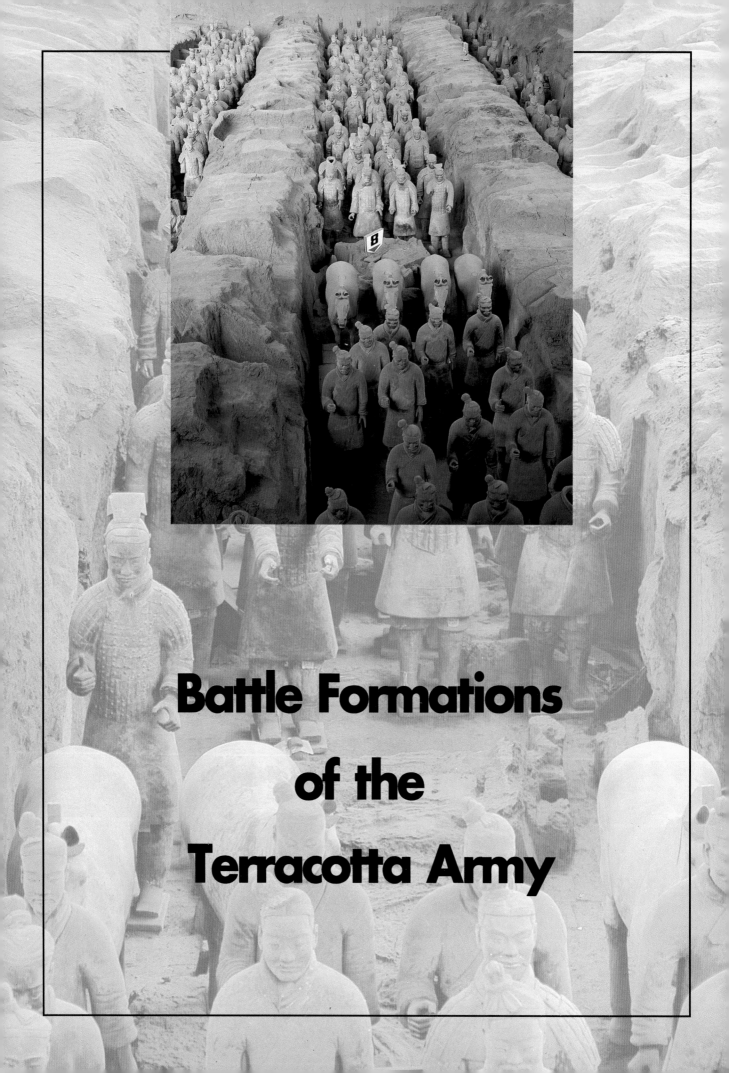

Battle Formations
of the
Terracotta Army

◀ Infantrymen closely following a war chariot.

Full view of the battle formation in Pit No. 1.

Full view of the battle formation in Pit No. 1.

1.
The vanguard formation in Pit No. 1.
2.
The vanguard formation in Pit No. 1.
3.
Back view of the vanguard formation in Pit No. 1.
4.
Left flank of the warriors in Pit No. 1.

4

1

2

3

1.

Back view of the battle formation in Pit No. 1.

2.

Rows of warriors separated by a wall.

3.

Right flank of the warriors in Pit No. 1.

4.

Infantrymen closely following a war chariot.

3

2

1

1.
The vanguard formation in Pit No. 1.

2.
Rows of armored infantrymen in Pit. No. 1.

3.
A section of the battle formation in Pit No. 1.

2

1

3

41

1.
Back view of a section of the battle formation in Pit No. 1.
2.
Armored infantry in front of a war chariot.
3.
Earthen walls in Pit No. 1.
4.
Chariot ruins in the pit.

2

◀ 4

3

1

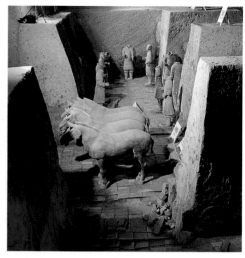

3

2

1

1.
Back view of armored infantrymen in Pit No. 1.
2.
Part of the battle formation in Pit No. 1.
3.
Chariot horses in Pit No. 3.
4.
Chariot garage in Pit No. 3.
5.
Southern chamber in Pit. No. 3.
6.
When the terracotta warriors were first uncovered,
many were in very poor condition.

4

5

6

2

3

4

1.
Armored infrantry at the back of a war chariot.
2.
Warriors in battle robes in front of a chariot.
3.
A four-horse war chariot in Pit No. 1.
4.
Warriors in battle robes preceding a war chariot.

4

1.
A war chariot and armored warriors in Pit No. 1.
2.
Drivers and chariot soldiers in Pit No. 1.
3.
Pit No. 3 — full view of the command headquarters of the underground army.
4.
Servicemen and guards in Pit. No. 3.

2

3

1

1.
Servicemen and guards in Pit No. 3.
2.
Part of Pit No. 3.
3.
A section of Pit No. 3.

1

2

3

1

2

1.
Part of the battle formation in Pit No. 1.
2.
A partial view of the battle formation in Pit. No. 1.

1.
Terracotta warriors freshly unearthed, battered and in pieces.
2.
The head and broken arms of a warrior.
3.
A beheaded warrior.

1.
Northern chember in Pit No. 3.
2.
Chariot ruins in the pit.
3.
Terracotta warriors freshly unearthed, battered
and in pieces.
4.
A four-horse war chariot with attending infantry.

Lifelike Statues

Warriors in battle robes.

63

3

1.
An armor-clad officer and his troops. ▶
2.
Another officer in armor.
3.
Terracotta soldier clad in armor.

2

1

2

1.
Terracotta soldiers clad in armor.
2.
Terracotta charioteer.

1.
Kneeling archer from Pit No. 2.
2.
Part of a kneeling archer.

2

1.
Terracotta soldier from Pit No. 3.
2.
Another terracotta soldier from Pit No. 3.
3.
Terracotta officer in armor. ▶
4.
Terracotta soldier clad in armor.

4

1.
Standing archer from Pit No. 2.
2.
Terracotta soldier clad in armor.
3.
Terracotta charioteer. ▶

2

1

1.
An officer clad in armor.
2.
One of the larger terracotta generals.
3.
Terracotta soldier clad in armor.

A terracotta general from Pit No. 2.

1.
Terracotta soldier clad in armor.
2.
Bust of a terracotta general.

1.
Back view of a terracotta general.

2.
A terracotta general.

3.
Bust of a terracotta general. ▶

1.
Terracotta soldier clad in armor.
2.
Rear view of a warrior in armor.
3.
Another officer clad in armor.
4.
Terracotta charioteer from Pit No. 3.
5.
Kneeling archer from Pit No. 2. ▶

Terracotta soldiers clad in armor. ▶

◀ Terracotta charioteer with gaunlets from Pit No. 2.

Another terracotta soldier clad in armor ▼

1

1.
A terracotta horse.
2.
The head of a terracotta horse.
3.
A chariot horse.

3

2

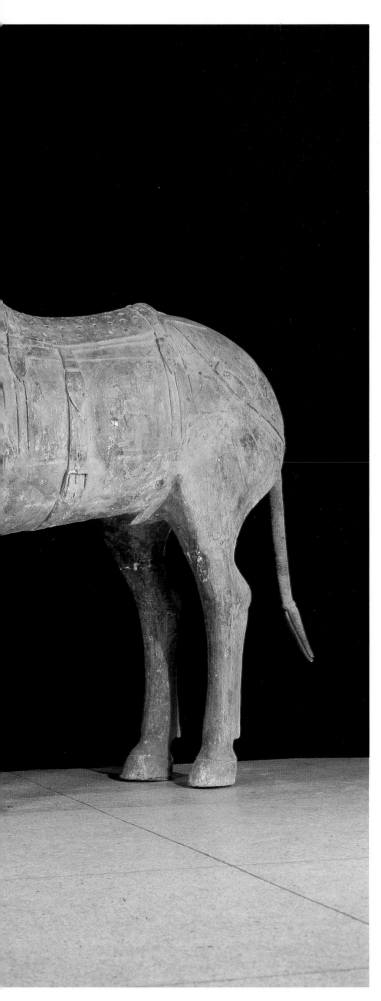

1.
Cavalryman and horse from Pit No. 2.
2.
Bust of a cavalryman.

A Great Variety of Vivid Facial Expressions

Exquisite Craftsmanship

with an Eye

for Detail

3

1.

◀ An ear.

2.

Eyes.

3.

A belt.

4.

Armor.

4

4

3

5

1.
A beard.
2.
Hair bun.
3.
A hand.
4.
Feet.
5.
Sole.

1

2

Threatening, Sharp Weapons

1.
Bronze *pi*s (a dagger of 30-odd centimeters long
with a flat stem at the end, affixed to a
3-meter-long wooden shaft to form a long weapon
to stab with, rather like a spear).
2.
A bronze lance.

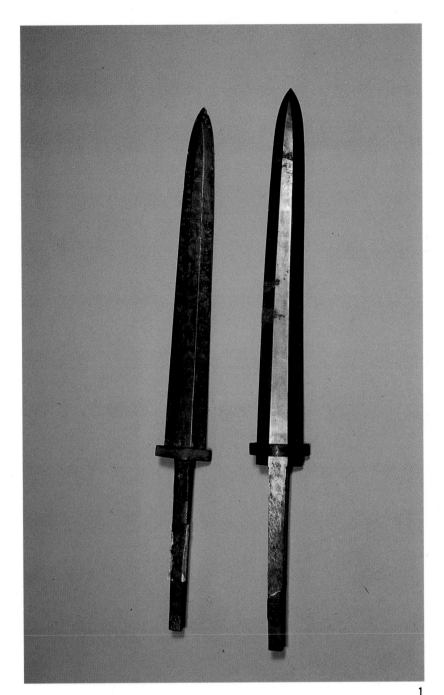

1

2

1.

A bronze spear.

2.

A crossbow trigger.

3.

Bronze swords.

4.

Arrow heads.

5.

A bunch of arrowheads freshly unearthed.

5

1

2

4

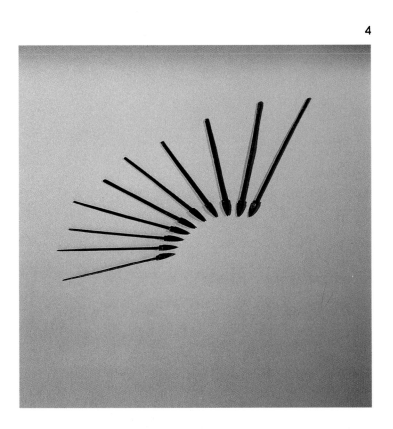

3

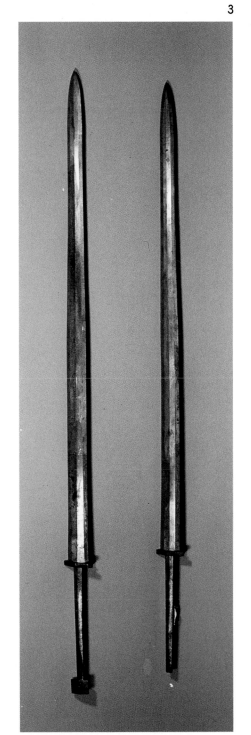

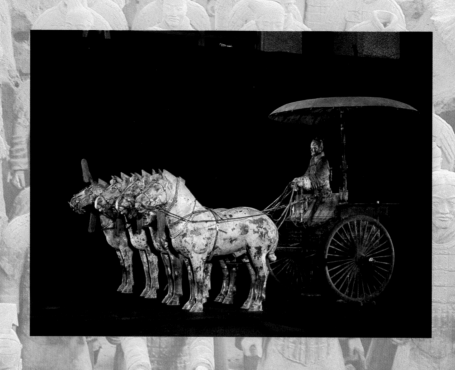

Bronze Chariots and Horses of Superb Craftsmanship

1.
Where the chariots and horses were discovered.
2.
◄ Detail of No. 1 bronze chariot.
3.
Charioteer of No. 1 bronze chariot.
4.
Bronze shield on No. 1 chariot.

1

4

3

1.

No. 2 bronze chariot and horses.

2.

Details of one of the horse heads.

3.

Designs on one of the bronze chariots.

1

3

2

117

1.
No. 1 bronze chariot and horses.
2.
Facial ornament of a horse.
3.
Girth worn by a horse around the belly.

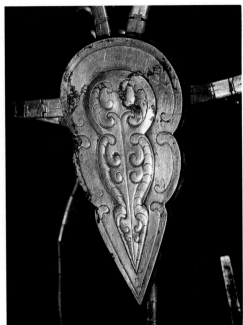

1

2

3

Detail of No. 2 bronze chariot.

Pottery figures of bowman on knees unearthed in the No.2 Pit.

Excavation of the No.2 Pit.

Pottery figure of bowman on knees in the No.2 Pit.

Pottery figure of cavalryman in the No.2 Pit.

Yang Zhifa, one of the finders of the terracotta figures.

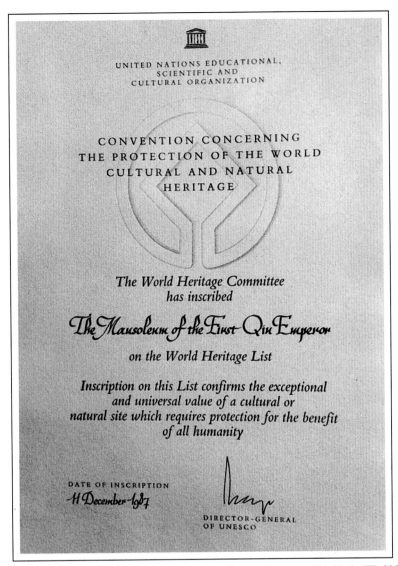

UNITED NATIONS EDUCATIONAL,
SCIENTIFIC AND
CULTURAL ORGANIZATION

CONVENTION CONCERNING
THE PROTECTION OF THE WORLD
CULTURAL AND NATURAL
HERITAGE

The World Heritage Committee
has inscribed

The Mausoleum of the First Qin Emperor

on the World Heritage List

Inscription on this List confirms the exceptional
and universal value of a cultural or
natural site which requires protection for the benefit
of all humanity

DATE OF INSCRIPTION
11 December 1987

DIRECTOR-GENERAL
OF UNESCO

In December 1987, the Qinshihuang Mausoleum (including the terrocotta warriors and horses) was listed in the "World Cultural Heritage" by the UNESCO.

图书在版编目（ＣＩＰ）数据

秦始皇帝地下大军团：世界第八奇迹 ＝ THE SUBTER-
RAN EAN ARMY OF EMPEROR QIN SHI HUANG：THE
EIGHTH WON DER OF THE WORLD：英文／. － 北京：中
国旅游出版社，1995.6 重印
ISBN 7 － 5032 － 0980 － 1

Ⅰ．秦… Ⅱ．①吴… ②郭… Ⅲ．秦始皇陵 － 兵马俑 － 摄
影集吴晓丛撰文；郭佑民摄影 Ⅳ．K878.9 － 64

中国版本图书馆 CIP 数据核字(95)第 06877 号

Editors-in-Chief: Wu Xiaocong,
Guo Youmin
Writer: Wu Xiaocong
Photographer: Guo Youmin
Editors: Yang Yin, Wu Jianqun
Designers: Wu Yue
Technical Editor: Liu Jinglin
English Translators: Tan Min, Zhang Siying,
Lee R. Thomas

Publisher: China Travel and Tourism Press

ISBN 7-5032-0980-1/G368
Third Print, October 1998
Publisher: China Travel and Tourism Press
Producer: Hua Tian International Tourism Advertising Co.
000006000

（英文版）